TULLY AND
THE NEW RULES

Available in the Tales of Tully series

Tully's Life
This heart-warming story follows the journey of Tully from street dog to much-loved family pet, teaching young readers about the importance of kindness, understanding and hope.

Tully Takes Off!
Tully has arrived in her new home with her new grown-up, but she does not like it one bit! When Tully sees an opportunity to go back to her old life on the streets - the only life she has known up to now - she takes it with both paws. With a search underway, it is up to her new grown-up to work out what Tully needs and help get her safely home.

Tully and the Sad Day
Tully has woken up feeling grey and cloudy inside and she does not know what to do. She cannot help her big feeling because she does not know what it is. As her different feelings begin to work together in the wrong way, it is up to Tully's grown-up to help her to understand what she needs.

Go To Sleep Tully!
It is night time and Tully is tired, but she does not want to go to sleep. Her new grown-up knows that Tully is trying every trick she can to avoid going go to bed! With lots of adventures planned and Tully needing her rest, Tully's grown-up needs to find a way to help Tully learn to not be so worried about bedtime.

Tully and the Midnight Feast
Tully is a newly-adopted dog settling in with her new grown-up. Since her arrival, her snacks have started mysteriously disappearing from the cupboard and appearing under her bed, she seems to have forgotten her manners, and there are days when she just cannot stop eating! Tully and her grown-up need to work together to help Tully with her worries about food.

Tully and the Scary Day
Tully has woken up feeling scared. She isn't really sure why, but today feels like a very scary day, and she just wants to hide. Tully's grown-up is thankfully there to help Tully manage her big feelings and see that the day is not so scary after all.

Don't Touch Tully!
Tully is settling in with her new grown-up. She has learned that the new grown-up is a safe person and she enjoys strokes and cuddles with them. Then Tully starts to meet new people, who want to show her how loved she is. Unfortunately, Tully doesn't feel the same about people she does not know and trust. It is up to Tully's grown-up to find a way to help Tully with her big feelings and to be Tully's voice, when she can't use hers.

Tully and the Tummy Ache
Tully has a tummy ache and it's making her feel quite grumpy. She doesn't want to eat or drink, and she can't get comfortable. Her tummy is sore and it's getting worse! Tully is in a toilet muddle. So, Tully and her grown-up work together to sort the muddle out and help Tully to cure her tummy ache.

Tully's Birthday

It's Tully's birthday, and her grown-up has planned a special day for her, but Tully doesn't feel like celebrating. As the day begins to unfold, so do Tully's big feelings. Tully doesn't know what to do about the big feelings, so she does a bad thing. Luckily, Tully's grown-up is there to help her feel better about herself, and enjoy the rest of her birthday.

Listen, Tully!

Tully does not always like to listen, especially when her grown-up is trying to stop her having fun. Tully decides that instead of listening, she can be in charge. But when things start to go wrong, Tully and her grown-up need to work out how Tully can begin to find listening a little bit easier.

Tully and the Makeover

Tully has been having lots of fun playing in the mud, but now her grown-up says she has to have a bath. Oh dear! Tully is not sure she wants one of those. She is feeling a bit nervous about what is going to happen to her, but Tully's grown-up shows her that there is nothing to worry about. Having a bath is a good thing after all.

Tully and Vera

Tully has moved in with her new grown-up but she is missing her foster carer, Vera. Tully is struggling to understand why she had to leave, and whether it is okay to have big feelings about Vera. It is up to Tully's grown-up to try and help her to understand loss and endings and why, sometimes, they have to happen to make space for new beginnings.

Tully and the Chase

Tully loves to be chased. It gives her a feeling of excitement which starts off as being fun, but one day the excited feeling suddenly and very quickly becomes a feeling which is too big. Instead of feeling excited, Tully starts to feel scared. Tully and her grown-up need to work out how they can play Tully's exciting game without it becoming a bit too much for her, and causing a muddle.

Tully at Christmas

Things are starting to feel a bit different in Tully's house and all around outside. Tully's grown-up looks different, strange lights are appearing everywhere and people have started putting their gardens indoors! Tully is not sure what to make of this thing called Christmas – she just wants everything to stay the same. What can Tully's grown-up do to make Christmas-time a nicer time for both of them?

Tully Goes on Holiday

Tully has gone on a holiday with her grown-up. After a difficult start, things seem to be going well. But when the fairground opens up, with all its flashing lights, loud music and food smells, Tully's big feelings get the better of her, making her want to run. And she does! Tully's grown-up needs to find her in time to show her that holidays can be fun after all.

Tully and the New Rules

Tully likes lots of things about living in a house with her grown-up, but one thing she really doesn't like is all the rules! Tully thinks the rules are all very boring and her grown-up must want to stop her from having fun. One day Tully breaks her least favourite rule, and something bad happens. Tully doesn't know what to do! Can Tully's grown-up get to the bottom of this muddle so it doesn't happen again?

Tully and the New Rules

TALES OF TULLY

Jess van der Hoech

JV Trauma Tools & Training

ISBN-13 978-1-06-87937-0-7
Editing by Sarah Ogden
www.jvtraumatools.co.uk

Acknowledgements

As always, to my trusted editor Sarah Ogden for all that you do to make these books come to life. I will never fully know what goes on behind the scenes, but it is a joy to work alongside you on these projects. Thank you.

Thank you to my supervisor Linda Hoggan for your continued support, encouragement, discussion and much-welcomed feedback on this series. I learn so much from you and the knowledge I have gained form our conversations has been invaluable across my practice, the books and now this series. Thank you.

Thank you to Laura Benham, for your support in giving me feedback, the searching questions, your friendship and of course, the countless conversations about dogs, the content of which has become quite useful! Thank you.

To the children and families who I meet in my therapy room, from whom I have learned more about hope and healing than any course could ever teach me. Your input, ideas, questions and answers are so valuable to me and I will be forever grateful. Thank you.

Preface

The *Tales of Tully* series is based on the adoption of an ex street dog from Bosnia who came to live with me in September 2023. Watching her try to settle and adapt from everything she had previously known to fit in with a new way of life began to present a number of ideas as to how to communicate such difficulties that can be experienced, to others who are in the process of adopting or who have adopted children. The aim of the series is to provide an opportunity to explore different situations, circumstances, feelings and experiences, finding new ways of communicating and understanding each other, through the voice of Tully.

Every home and every family will have a different set of rules and expectations to follow. While this is what makes a family unique, it can also be confusing, particularly for children who have lived in other – perhaps many – different families before. Consequences for a particular action in one home may have been ignored in another. There may have been no rules at all, or there may have been many.

Adjusting to a new environment can take time and can be particularly challenging for both adults and children. Any new people added into an environment can change the dynamic of what has existed so far, so understanding what the expectations are is of great importance.

When Tully first came home to me, I wanted her to know that I was the person who loved her the most in the world. I wanted to make up for all of the horrible experiences she had had in the past, and I wanted her to love me. In the beginning, I pretty much let her dictate how our lives were going to look. I quickly learned, however, that this was the worst idea, especially when she wanted me to chase her around the garden for fun – at midnight!

Tully needed rules and routines. I needed to be the one to be in charge of those rules. We could compromise at times, but ultimately, I needed to be 'Top Dog', even though she wanted to be. If I had given in to her, the message I would actually be giving would be 'You can be in charge, Tully, because I cannot keep you safe', which was the opposite of what I wanted to create. In order to be the boss, I needed to be in charge of the rules, but importantly, the consequences of a rule break always needed to be the same. This was how I was going to become predictable and what was ultimately going to create a sense of inherent safety in Tully.

It is the same with children. They need to know what the rules are, that the rules are there to keep them safe and that consequences will be linked to that particular rule break, in order for it to make sense. Consequences need to be predictable in order to encourage the confidence in them to be able to tell the truth, as they will know what the outcome will be.

How to use this book

First and foremost, ensure that both you and the child are well-regulated and comfortable when you begin to read Tully's story. Make sure you choose a time when you are unlikely to be interrupted. The child may like a soother, a favourite or fidget toy, a drink or something to suck or chew to help them to stay regulated.

If the child is calm, then begins to try and distract or move away from the reading, make a note of what they have just heard in the text. It is very likely that they will have just provided you with some valuable information about something that they cannot tolerate or want to avoid for now.

The questions have been designed not only to explore the internal world of the child, but to help to develop a common language between the child and adult who are using this book together. The child cannot get the answers to the questions incorrect. Their interpretation of the thoughts and feelings Tully is having may provide some very significant information about the child's own thoughts and feelings. The child may want to expand the answers to talk about themselves and may even be able to make comparisons between Tully's feelings and their own.

Tully and the New Rules

Tully was feeling bored and restless. She had been settling into her new home for a few months and she was starting to like it there. Tully had moved into a new home with a new grown-up after living as a street and shelter dog in Bosnia for most of her life.

Tully had lots of things to learn about living in a house. She had not had a safe house before and she needed to learn how everything about living in a house worked, including routines, dinner times, exercise times, play times and bed times.

What else might Tully need to learn about living in a safe house?

What routines do you have in your house?

What makes your house safe?

Tully also had been learning a lot about her new grown-up. She knew her grown-up liked to give her healthy food, to cuddle her, to sit with her while she fell asleep and the grown-up talked in a calm voice, most of the time. She also knew that her grown-up liked things called 'rules'.

What rules do you have in your house?

Do you have rules anywhere outside the house?

How do you feel about having rules?

When Tully had lived as a street dog by herself, she had not had to follow any rules at all. Tully could look after herself! Some of the rules in her new home were a bit boring and Tully couldn't understand why she had to follow them.

"Zoomies are only for the garden," was Tully's least favourite rule. Tully loved to zoomie – running and spinning in circles as fast as she could – what fun!

Why has Tully's grown-up made rules for Tully to follow?

Should Tully follow the rules? Why?

It was raining outside, so Tully hadn't been out for her walk yet. She had lots of energy stuck inside her body and she wanted to get it out.

Tully's grown-up was upstairs. Tully really wanted to do just one quick zoomie. She did one, then another and another, up on the sofa, down again, spinning and twirling – she was having a lovely time.

Until…..CRASH! Tully accidentally knocked over a vase of flowers. The vase smashed and there was water all over the floor. Oh dear!

How does Tully feel now?

What might her grown-up say?

Tully's grown-up came rushing downstairs. "What happened here?" the grown-up asked. Tully was lying on the sofa pretending to be fast asleep.

"Did you do this Tully?" the grown-up asked.

Tully pretended to wake up just then and she stared at the vase, pretending to be confused.

Why might Tully be doing this?

What might Tully be worried might happen if her grown-up knew she had broken the vase?

Tully's grown-up started to clean up the mess. Tully had lots of big feelings about what had happened. She had already had big feelings because of all the energy she needed to use up. She had a big happy feeling as she did zoomies in the lounge, then she got more big feelings when the vase broke and her grown-up came and saw it.

What big feelings might Tully have had?

Tully's grown-up finished cleaning up the broken vase and came and sat beside Tully on the sofa. The grown-up held her paw.

"Tully, I wonder if you were doing zoomies in the lounge and that was how the vase was broken?"

How does Tully feel about her grown-up knowing the truth about the vase?

Tully looked at the floor and started to cry.

"I thought so," the grown-up said. "I wonder if you got big feelings because you did not know what I would do if you broke a rule. I wonder if you were worried that you would be in trouble and you did not know what that trouble would be?"

Could Tully's grown-up be right?

Are there other reasons why Tully did not want to tell the truth?

"We have rules to keep us safe Tully," said the grown-up. "I do not want you to get hurt inside the house if things get broken when you are running around. That is why we only do zoomies outside. Let me check your paws and make sure you do not have any broken bits of vase in them."

How does Tully feel now that she knows her grown-up does not want her to get hurt?

"I know when you were young, you did not have to follow any rules and it must be hard for you to learn to follow rules now. The rules we have are to keep you safe and it is important that you follow them," her grown-up said.

Tully had not realised that the rules were there to help her. Tully had thought that the rules were because her grown-up was boring and did not want her to have any fun.

Does Tully feel differently about the rules now?

What rules might Tully make if she could be in charge?

Tully started to learn that even though she found it tricky sometimes, she should try her best to follow the rules. If she did break a rule, she knew that her grown-up would help her and she could always tell her grown-up the truth. Tully is safe now.

About the author

Jess van der Hoech is a qualified therapist who has spent the last ten years studying and working with the impact of developmental trauma and, in particular, the assessment and treatment of children and adolescents with complex trauma and dissociation.

As well as supporting birth families, Jess works with looked-after and adopted children and families, using skills in attachment-focused therapy and therapeutic parenting techniques.

Jess is a supervisor, trainer and motivational speaker with a passion for writing therapeutic books that are accessible to children and families to help with the healing process and to increase awareness in the impact of trauma.

Also by Jess van der Hoech

What A Muddle (2016) ISBN 978 18381987 0 1 (Co-authored with Renée Potgieter Marks)
An interactive, practical workbook designed to help children who have difficulties with emotional regulation to begin to understand what is happening in their bodies. A variety of activities throughout the book enable the child to start to explore these ideas through the story of Sam, while gently encouraging them to begin to verbalise their own experiences. Carrying out the physical exercises in the book can promote changes in emotional regulation. The text is written in a child-friendly, gender-neutral style, and is easy to understand for parents, carers and practitioners alike. For children aged 4-12.

These Three Words (2018) ISBN 978 18381987 5 6
Also available as an e-book. A unique therapeutic novel for teenagers with the aim of linking together the feelings, emotions and behaviours connected to anxiety, with some of the therapeutic tools that can be used in order to enable better self-regulation, increased confidence and different ways of thinking. The book is equally valuable to parents of teenagers with anxiety, giving them an insight and understanding into some of the issues that may be affecting their child, and potentially opening up a line of communication and a way forward between parent and teen.

These Three Words: The Journal (2019) ISBN 978 18381987 2 5
A thought-provoking and hands-on workbook, combining a series of practical exercises and tools designed to assist teenagers who are struggling with the symptoms of anxiety. Addressing the anxious responses in both brain and body, this journal provides the reader with the opportunity to discover therapeutic coping techniques and learn how to apply them to their own personal problem areas, before committing to a twenty-eight-day practice to promote good emotional regulation and reduced anxiety. The journal can be used alongside the therapeutic novel These Three Words, or as a standalone workbook, and it is suitable for use by the teenage reader on their own, with a parent, or in a group.

Beastie, Baby and the Brand-New Mummy (2022) ISBN 978 18381987 3 2 and *Beastie, Baby and the Brand-New Daddy (2022) ISBN 978 18381987 4 9*
A therapeutic story that looks at the external signs of pathological dissociation in a child. Dolly's story helps children who have experienced early trauma to begin to understand, in a very simple way, what dissociation is and why it has happened in their internal world. Tools and techniques are included within the story that parents and caregivers can use to assist the child in the first stages of their healing process. Beautiful illustrations on every page enhance the story of Dolly, and help the reader to relate to the events that happen, to notice the methods Dolly has developed to manage her feelings, and to think about what is happening in their own internal world. For children aged 4-12

Printed in Great Britain
by Amazon